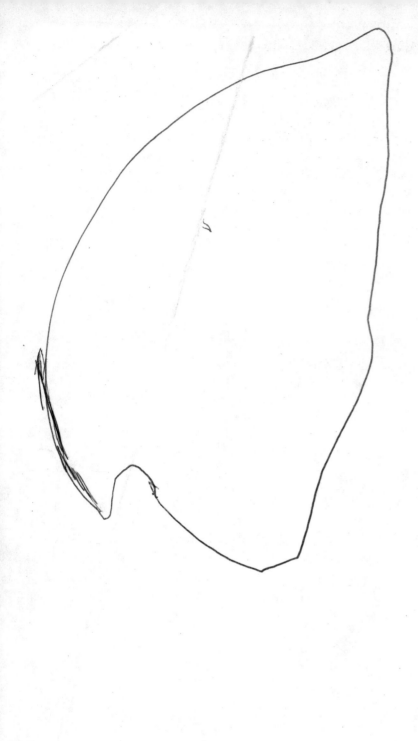

AlphaBasiCs

SCHOOL

 from to

Bobbie Kalman

Crabtree Publishing Company

AlphaBasiCs

Created by Bobbie Kalman

**In memory of my father
Imre Kalman (1921-1999)
May you find peace!**

Author and Editor-in-Chief
Bobbie Kalman

Managing editor
Lynda Hale

Editor
Jane Lewis

Copy editors
John Crossingham
Heather Levigne

Computer design
Lynda Hale
John Crossingham

Production coordinator
Hannelore Sotzek

Consultant
Joan King

Special thanks to
The Hill family; Samantha Crabtree; the staff and students of the National Ballet School; the staff and students of Michael J. Brennan and Pine Grove Elementary Schools; Victoria Village Public School; Armour Heights Public School; Jackie Stafford and the students of Elmlea Junior School; Ramona Gellel and the students of Precious Blood School; the students of Eggert Road Elementary School; Moorelands Camp; all the children in other photographs

Photographs
Marc Coaté: page 27; Marc Crabtree: pages 9 (all), 18 (top & bottom left), 20 (both), 26 (left), 28 (right), 30 (top, bottom right); Peter Crabtree: page 14 (right); Christl Hill: pages 14 (top left), 15 (left); Bobbie Kalman: pages 7, 14 (bottom left), 15 (top & bottom right), 18 (right), 31 (center); other images by Digital Stock and Eyewire, Inc.

Illustrations
Barbara Bedell: borders and all illustrations except title page, pages 12 and 29; Brian Franczak: page 12; Cori Marvin: page 29

Crabtree Publishing Company

350 Fifth Avenue
Suite 3308
New York
N.Y. 10118

360 York Road, RR 4
Niagara-on-the-Lake
Ontario, Canada
L0S 1J0

73 Lime Walk
Headington
Oxford OX3 7AD
United Kingdom

Cataloging in Publication Data

Kalman, Bobbie
  School from A to Z

(AlphaBasiCs)
Includes index.

ISBN 0-86505-388-X (library bound) ISBN 0-86505-418-5 (pbk.)
This book is an alphabetical introduction to various aspects of school, such as "Class," "Homework," "Library," and "Teacher."

1. Education, Elementary—Juvenile literature. 2. Schools—Juvenile literature. [1. Schools. 2. Alphabet.]
I. Title. II. Series: Kalman, Bobbie. AlphaBasiCs.

LB1556.K35 1999   j372   LC 99-22340
                                        CIP

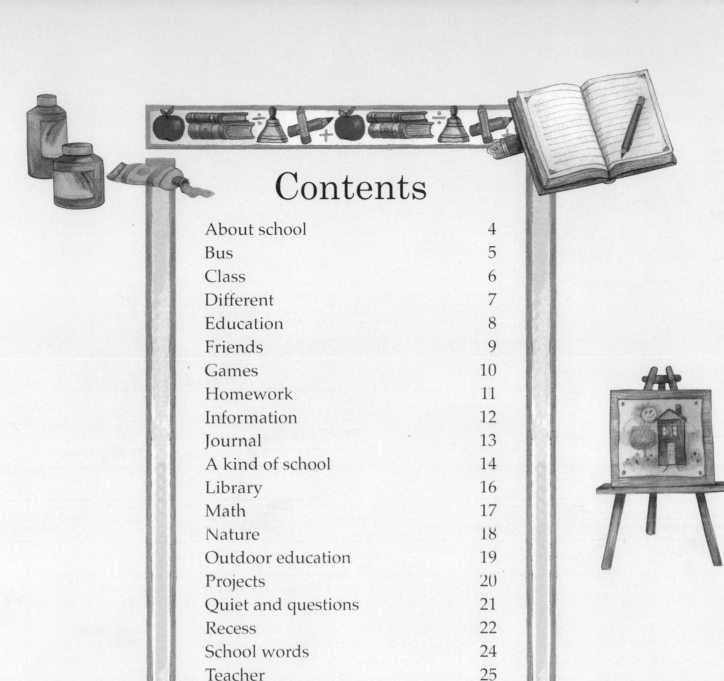

Contents

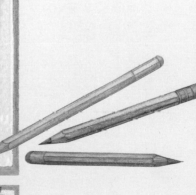

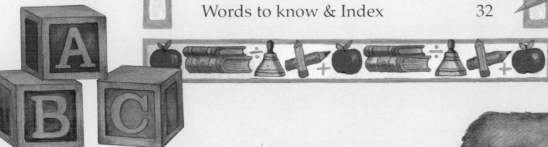

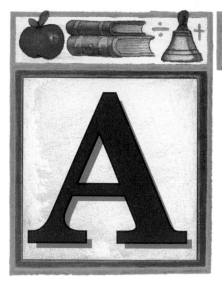

lot of words **about school** begin with A. I **attend** school five days a week. I learned the **alphabet**, and I am learning how to **add**. I pay **attention** to the teacher. I **ask** her for help when I have trouble doing an **activity**. On a sheet of paper, write all the words on this page that start with A.

Ask me! I put up my hand when I want to answer a question.

I absolutely adore art!

B

is for **bus**. I go to school in a school bus. The driver's name is Betty, and she picks me up after breakfast. I board the bus and buckle my seat belt. Betty brings many kids to school. We arrive just before the bell rings. I say "bye" to Betty and begin my busy day at school.

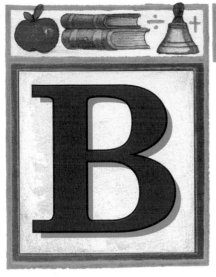

Make a list of the words on this page that begin with B. Think of five other B words and use all the words to write a story about your busy day at school.

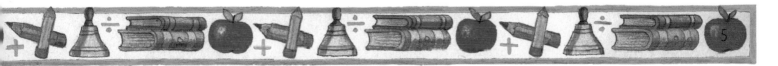

C

is for **class**. I am in Mr. Cole's class. Mr. Cole is a cool teacher. This morning he drew some cats on the board with chalk. I copied the cats and colored them with my pencil crayons. In the afternoon I worked at the computer center. I learned how to create crazy shapes with the mouse!

Draw a picture of five C words found on this page.

D

is for **different**. No one is exactly like me. We are all different, and we are all special! Debbie is good at sports, and Dave is a fast reader. I need help with math, but I work hard! We are all good at different things. How are you the same as your friends? How are you different?

is for **education**. I go to school to get an excellent education. In elementary school, I learn skills such as math and spelling. When I go to high school, I will study hard so I can get good grades and become an engineer like my mother. I have to attend university to become an engineer.

(above) I am learning how to use the computer at school. (top right) My sister Evi is in high school. (bottom) Ellen, my stepsister, is graduating from university. She studied English and hopes to become a writer. What would you like to do after you finish your education?

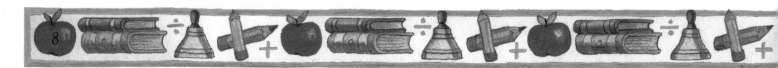

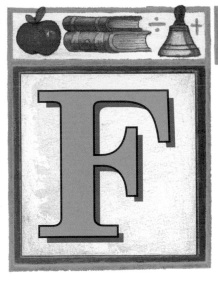

is for **friends**. There are a lot of things I like about school, but being with my friends is my favorite. My friends and I hang out and talk or play games. Sometimes we disagree with one another and have a fight. We don't argue for long, though. We shake hands and say, "Sorry."

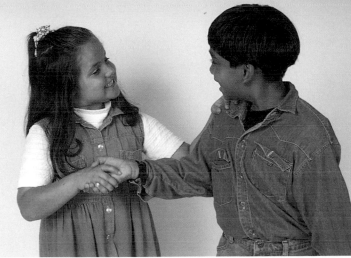

(above) Hanging around the schoolyard is fun when my friends are with me. We talk about all kinds of things.
*(left) On Friday, our friends Fred and Francine had a fight about which game they would play at recess. How do you think they reached a **compromise**?*

G

is for **games**. I like playing games and sports with my friends. We play great games in gym class, like dodgeball and soccer. Sometimes we learn gymnastics. Today, my brother Greg's class played with big, colorful balls in the gymnasium. How many G words are on this page?

I am in grade two. Our class pet is a goldfish named Gus. I giggle when he makes goofy fish faces. Do you have a pet in your classroom? Is it a goat, a gorilla, or a gigantic giraffe who is good at art?

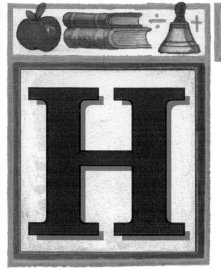

is for **homework**, which does not make me happy! If I do not finish my work at school, I have to take it home. Sometimes it is too hard. Dad helps me with reading, and Mom helps me with math. After my homework is done, I play with my hamster, Harry. He is hilarious!

Harry often hides. Come here, Harry!

Hannah and Hilary have heaps of homework today. They won't be going out to play!

My father helps me when I need a hand with my homework. How many H words are on this page?

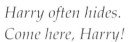

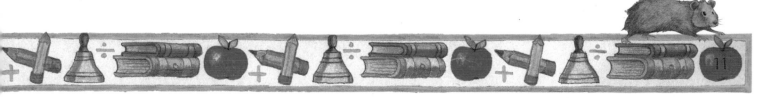

I

is for **information**. In school I learn important information. I learn about animals and plants. I learn about people who live in other places. I am interested in investigating dinosaurs. I use my imagination to pretend I am living in the time of the dinosaurs! How do you use your imagination?

*These two dinosaurs were called Protoceratops. They were the **ancestors** of later dinosaurs called Triceratops, which had three horns.*

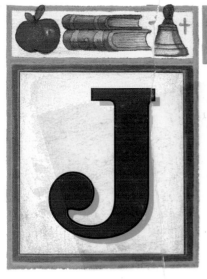

is for journal. I write in my journal every day. I write about the things I do and the things I learn. If I am worried about something, I write about it, and I feel better. When I write about happy things, I feel just plain jolly! What makes you feel happy, worried, or sad?

Does your class have a journal time? What do you write about in your journal? Each day I write down five things for which I feel thankful. Counting my blessings fills me with joy!

K is for a different **kind** of school. Most kids go to a public or private school, but I don't go to a school at all. I am getting a great education at home! I live on a sailboat with my parents and brother. We sail to many exciting places. My parents are my teachers, and the world is my school!

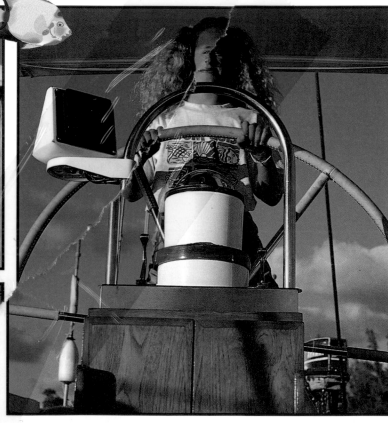

*(top left) When I visit different countries, I learn about geography and history. I have traveled since I was a baby. (left) Each day my mother teaches me reading, writing, and math. (above) My father teaches me how to **navigate** and sail the boat. I can read maps and **charts** and calculate how long it will take us to arrive at our next stop.*

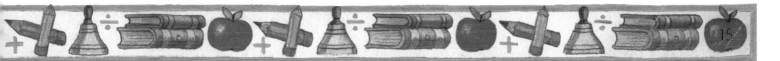

Each morning I spend three hours on my lessons. I read books and write stories on the computer. In the afternoons we do exciting things such as **helmet diving**! I can walk on the ocean floor and see lots of colorful fish! (right)

(above and top right) Big fish, little fish.
Living on a boat helps me learn a lot about fish!
Today I helped my brother catch a big one for dinner.

(right) Wherever I go, I collect flowers and dry them. I
look them up in a book about flowers and learn their names.

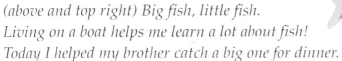

is for **library**. Do you like reading books? I do. Libraries lend books. The librarian helps me find **non-fiction** books for reports and projects. Non-fiction books have information to help me learn. **Fiction** books are made-up stories. I like all kinds of books. Books are lovely!

Last week my friends and I went to the library to do a report on lakes and rivers. I looked at lots of books and took three home. I returned them all on time. Write down the names of the last three books you borrowed from the library. Which is the best book you have ever read?

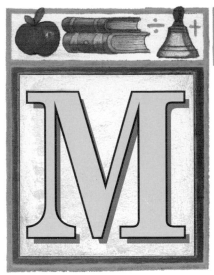

is for **math**, which is short for mathematics. We learn about numbers in math class. I practice skills such as adding, subtracting, multiplying, and dividing. Math helps me count money and calculate how much I need to go to the movies. Make a list of the many ways you use math.

I use math to measure the size and weight of different objects. I also use my math skills to draw graphs on the computer. Learning math takes practice!

is for **nature**. My teacher takes our class outdoors to learn about nature. She gives us a list of things to find. We carry a notebook and magnifying glass to help us do our work. We collect leaves from the ground—we never pull them off the trees! Sometimes we find bugs. We love bugs!

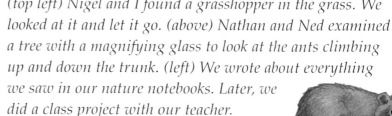

(top left) Nigel and I found a grasshopper in the grass. We looked at it and let it go. (above) Nathan and Ned examined a tree with a magnifying glass to look at the ants climbing up and down the trunk. (left) We wrote about everything we saw in our nature notebooks. Later, we did a class project with our teacher.

O

is for **outdoor** education. Sometimes we go to an outdoor-education center to learn about nature. We stay overnight in tents or cabins and cook our own food. During the day, we study the plants, rocks, and water. We play games and learn how to live in the wilderness.

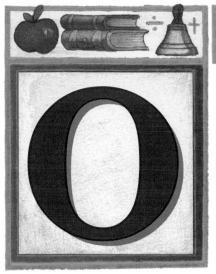

(above) "I found a frog!" (top right) It is fun to sleep in a tent. I am sharing my tent with Olaf. (right) My friends Oprah and Olivia went rock climbing with me. Write a story about an outdoor experience you have had.

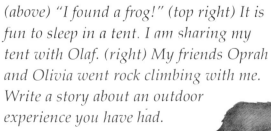

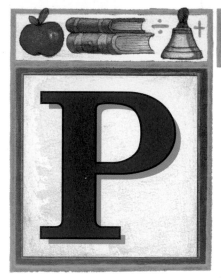

P is for **projects**. I love doing projects! Projects are creative and fun. We get to draw and paint, and we learn a lot, too. This month we made musical instruments for a class party. We played music and ate popcorn, potato chips, and Mrs. Pepe's pecan pie, which was particularly pleasant.

(left) We used paper and straws to make a **pan flute**, *bottles and peas for* **maracas**, *and wood, nails, and rubber bands to construct a* **zither**. *Patrice wore a pineapple hat!*
(below) I researched my project about pets with a partner.

is for **quiet** and **questions**. I work quietly in class so others can work, too. I ask questions when I don't understand something. I use the words who, what, where, how, and why to ask a question. My teacher asks questions, too. I put up my hand quickly when I know the answer.

Do the children in your class keep quiet when the teacher is talking? Why do you think it is important to work quietly in class?

Asking questions helps me learn. What kind of questions do you ask in class? Ask five questions about school using each of the words who, what, where, how, and why.

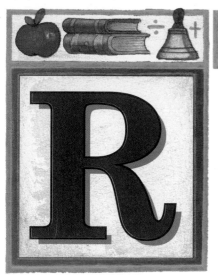

R is for **recess**. It is recess time! It is time to alk and laugh and run and jump and kick a ball and spin around and breathe fresh air and whoop and holler and play games with my friends.

I can dance and sing or skip and climb or roll some marbles or hang for a time—on an old tire with my friends. I can show off my skills on the jungle gym or recite a clapping rhyme. "Watch me hide!" No one can see inside, as I barrel down the tunnel slide!

WHEW!

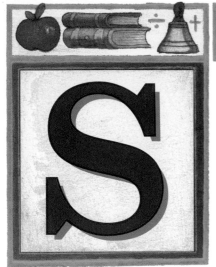

S is for **school**. I study many subjects in school, but science and social studies are my favorites. In social studies, we learn how people lived long ago. Sometimes we dress like pioneers. Look at our outfits! In science I learn about animals and plants. Using a microscope, I can see tiny things.

There are many school words that start with the letter S. Write sentences using all the words in the list below. Can you think of some more? Draw a picture to go with each word!

study   spelling
science   students
scissors   stencil
school spirit sports
social studies skills

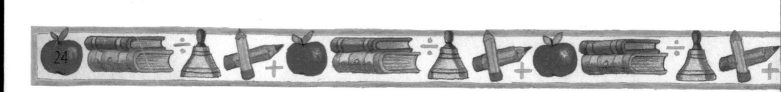

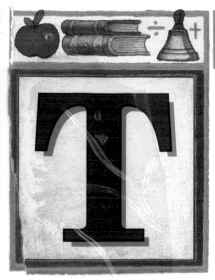

is for **teacher**. My teacher is terrific! Her name is Ms. Tate. She teaches us many interesting things and tells us we are talented. She sets up activity centers and helps us with our work. She watches us at recess to make sure we play safely. I always try to do my best! Thank you, Ms. Tate.

is for **uniforms**. In some schools, students wear uniforms. Everyone at my school wears one. Uniforms can be any color, but sometimes they are the school colors. I like wearing a uniform because I always know what to wear when I get up in the morning. Do you wear a **uniform**?

(left) Uma and her friends wear a uniform to school every day.

(below) I don't wear a uniform at school, but I wear one when I play soccer. Our team colors are red and white. Maybe they should be red, white, and dirty brown!

is for **vacation**. I love summer vacation! I get a break from school. Sometimes my family goes on a trip. Last year we visited Aunt Vera in Venezuela. My friend Victor went to camp. At the end of summer, I was ready to go back to school. I couldn't wait to be in the third grade!

W is for people who **work** at school. The principal the head of the school. She hires the teachers who teach us all day long. The office workers answer the phone and check the attendance sheets. The nurse takes care of us when we are sick. Custodians keep the school clean. Who works at your school?

Sometimes our principal greets us at the front door of our school. She knows the name of every student!

Our librarian is also called the learning-resources teacher. She teaches classes and shows us how to find information for our projects.

is for **xylophone** and other musical instruments. At school, we have a musical instrument class. Some students play recorders or drums. Xaviera plays a xylophone called a **marimba**. I play the violin. Do you play an instrument? Which one?

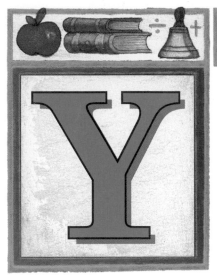

is for **your school**. What makes your school great? Do you jump for joy when you get there each day? Do you play games? Make a **yearbook** about your school. Draw pictures or take photographs of your classmates and write stories and poems about your favorite school activities.

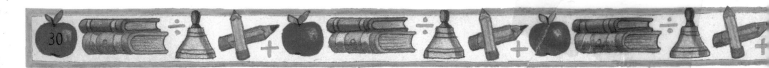

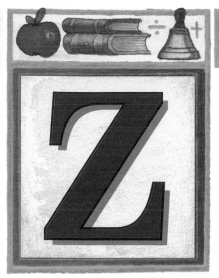

Z is for **zany**. Zany means silly. Sometimes my friends and I like to act zany at school. We asked our teacher if we could have a zany day every month. We wear zany makeup, make zany faces, and write zany stories. Acting zany makes us happy, and it makes the teacher laugh, too.

Is Zane in pain?

"Is your name Tara?" Zeb asks Zara!

Here's Zzzzoey!

Zsa Zsa is ga-ga about the zigzags on her forehead!

Gadzooks! Zeke's zuch a zilly!

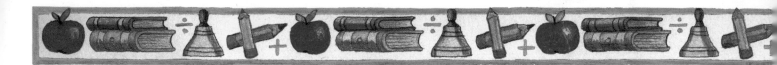

Words to know

calculate To figure out an answer
chart A map of the sea that shows currents and water depth
compromise An agreement in which each side gives in a little
custodian A caretaker; a person who cleans and maintains the school
fiction A story that is not true
graduate To complete one level of school, such as high school
graph A diagram that compares numbers
helmet diving Walking under water while wearing a helmet filled with air
maraca A hollow instrument filled with beans or stones

marimba A large xylophone with wooden bars
navigate To plan a boat's route, or to sail a boat along its route
non-fiction Information that is true
pan flute A musical instrument with tubes of different lengths
project A task students are given to help them learn
social studies The study of community, environment, geography, and history
xylophone A musical instrument with bars that play different notes when struck
zither A musical instrument with many strings that are picked to make sounds

Index

1 2 3 4 5 6 7 8 9 0   Printed in the U.S.A.   8 7 6 5 4 3 2 1 0 9